es of Survival

FIONA BEDDALL

Level 3

Series Editors: Andy Hopkins and Jocelyn Potter

Pearson Education Limited
Edinburgh Gate, Harlow,
Essex CM20 2JE, England
and Associated Companies throughout the world.

ISBN: 978-1-4082-2106-8

This edition first published by Pearson Education Ltd 2011

1 3 5 7 9 10 8 6 4 2

Text copyright © Fiona Beddall 2011
Illustrations by Terence Hand

Set in 11/14pt Bembo
Printed in China
SWTC/01

Published by Pearson Education Limited in association with
Penguin Books Ltd, and both companies being subsidiaries of Pearson PLC

Acknowledgements
The publisher would like to thank the following for their kind permission
to reproduce their photographs:

Corbis: Bettmann 4, Icon SMI / Christophe Dupont Elise 34; Press Association Images:
.com: 30

Every effort has been made to trace the copyright holders and we apologise in advance
for any unintentional omissions. We would be pleased to insert the appropriate
acknowledgement in any subsequent edition of this publication.

La presente publica ... oficial establecida por el Poder E... ativo
Nacional de la Repúb ... robada po ... el Expte.

For a comple ... ders series please go to
www.penguinr... write to your local Pearson...
or to: P... son Readers Marketing Depa... ment, Pearson Education,
Edinburgh Gate, Harlow, Essex C... 120 2JE, England.

Contents

Introduction

He could not walk. But he could pull and push himself along the ground with one arm and one leg.

This book tells eight of the world's greatest survival stories. From the cold of Antarctica to the heat of the Sahara Desert, from the endless water of the Atlantic Ocean to the tight space of a Rwandan bathroom, the people in these pages have faced death and survived. Some chose a life of danger and adventure. Others found themselves in danger while they were living ordinary lives. But they all have a story that is not easily forgotten.

These true stories cover almost five hundred years of history. Some tell of a lost world—for example, a bear attack in the land of the Native Americans*, before white people built towns and cities and railroads. Others, like the suffering and fear brought by a volcano, are timeless. Travel and the dangers of travel change over the years. In the 1520s, a ship hits rocks. In the 1970s, a plane crashes into the rain forest. But the needs of survivors are mostly the same: water, food, and a way to get home.

What makes the difference between survival and death? The first and most important answer is luck. The ocean pulls a man toward land, not away from it. Rescuers find him when he is still alive, not twenty-four hours too late. But for most of the people in these pages, survival was not only the result of luck. They were able to think calmly in the face of danger. They could eat things that make most people sick. And they could follow a plan, even when all hope was lost. They did not wait patiently for death. They fought it at every step.

★ Native Americans: the people who lived in North America before the arrival of Europeans

Serrano saw some big turtles climbing out of the ocean onto the beach.

An Island of Sand

After a long, hard swim, Pedro Serrano fell onto a beach, tired but alive. There was no sign now of his broken ship, lost under the waves. He waited for other sailors from the ship to arrive on the island. But no one came.

The next morning Serrano looked around the island that saved his life. It was a good size—a walk of many hours from one end to the other. But it was made of sand. There were no plants on it, no pools or rivers. His new home was a desert.

All hope now left him. It was the 1520s. Spanish ships visited the Caribbean regularly, but the ocean was very big and this island was small and unimportant. He probably had a wait of many years before any ships passed his way.

"My friends from the ship were lucky," he thought. "Their deaths in the waves were quick." He could imagine his own death on this desert island—slow, painful, lonely.

But he pushed away these fears. He needed food and drink ... soon. After some searching, he found some shellfish and insects. He ate them uncooked. He had no way to light a fire.

Later that day Serrano saw some big turtles climbing out of the ocean onto the beach. He ran toward them and quickly turned them onto their backs. Their legs danced in the air. He cut into their skin with the knife that he always kept in his belt. Then he drank their blood thirstily. He cut the meat out of their shells and dried it in the sun. Later he used the big shells to catch rainwater. Maybe he could survive on this desert island.

After a few weeks he had plenty of dried turtle meat and water. He now wanted a fire. "Passing ships won't rescue me if I can't make any smoke," he thought. Sometimes the waves carried wood to the island. But how could he light it? At home in Spain, he could start a fire with stones and a knife. But here

1

he had no stones. Was a fire impossible?

Not for Serrano. He swam out from the island and looked underwater for stones. Day after day he searched. Finally ... success! He found a good pile of stones and carried them back to the island, a few at a time. He broke one against another until they had sharp corners. Then he cut part of his shirt into small pieces. He held his knife under the pieces of shirt, and hit it again and again with the stones. This lit the pieces of shirt, and the shirt lit the wood. At last he had a fire.

He fed his fire carefully with things from the beach. He built a shelter with the largest turtle shells to keep the rain off it. Now he just had to wait for a ship.

He did not have to wait many months. He saw one ship, then another. But the smoke from his fire did not bring anyone to the island. Maybe no one saw the smoke, or maybe they were too afraid of the dangerous rocks in the area. Months passed, then years. Serrano began to lose all hope of rescue.

♦

About three years after his arrival on the island, Serrano was asleep. It was a quiet night. There were no signs that his life on the island was changing. But, unknown to Serrano, a ship was in trouble not far away. Soon it was destroyed on rocks. Its only survivor swam to Serrano's island and, in the morning, saw the smoke from a fire. "My friends from the ship are here, too," he thought happily, walking toward the smoke.

But the sailor did not find his friends. He found Serrano—a strange animal, like a man but wild, without clothes, and covered in long hair. He was very scared.

When Serrano saw a man coming toward him, he was scared, too. "He's a trick of the mind. I'm going mad!" he thought. He ran from the sailor, crying, "Help me, Jesus!"

When the sailor heard the word *Jesus*, his fear of the wild man left him. "Come back, brother," he called. "We are of the same religion!" But Serrano did not stop running.

The race continued for some time. But finally Serrano accepted that the man was real. He realized that they were both in the same hopeless position. He threw his arms around his new friend and tears ran down his face.

In the following months the two men lived together. They passed their days looking for food and firewood. They organized their shells of rainwater and, most importantly, they watched the fire, day and night. "If the fire goes out, no one will ever rescue us," explained Serrano.

But soon they had a disagreement. Each man felt that the other was not doing enough of the work. Angrily, they decided to live in different parts of the island. For months they did not speak. Finally, though, they realized their stupidity. They made friends again, and lived together for the next four years.

Other ships passed, but still no rescuers came. They decided that their only future was on their lonely island. Often they hoped for death. But then, when all hope of rescue was gone, a ship saw their smoke. The ship sent a boat to look around. The two men danced in excitement as the boat came near.

The sailors on the boat started to worry. What were these crazy, hairy things on the beach? They turned their boat around, away from danger. Just in time, Serrano and his friend cried, "In the name of Jesus, help us!" Less scared now, the rescuers came for them.

Soon the two hairy men were enjoying food and drink on their rescuers' ship. They told everyone the story of their adventures. It felt wonderful to have company again.

Sadly for Serrano, his friend died on his way home to Europe, but Serrano arrived safely in Spain. He became quite famous for his adventures, and he died a rich man.

Attacked by a Bear

The American West* was a dangerous place for white people in 1823. Near the Missouri River, Hugh Glass and his friends were looking for animal skins that they could sell at home in the East. But their trip was not going well. Seventeen of them were already dead—killed in two different Native American attacks in the last few weeks.

They moved as quickly and quietly as possible, fearing another attack. They always stayed in a group.

But Hugh Glass did not always like the company of others. One afternoon he decided to walk through the woods alone. Suddenly he saw a grizzly bear—a mother with three babies. As Glass lifted his gun to the bear, she ran toward him. She stood up on her back legs, two meters tall. Glass shot at her. The bear was hurt, but still she attacked him with her front legs. He fell to the ground, screaming. She bit him and hit him, but she was losing blood. Soon she was dead, on top of Glass.

Some of his friends heard Glass's screams. They came running. When they saw the dead bear with a man's body under it, they thought the worst—another dead friend. They could not believe it when they pushed the bear away. Glass was still alive.

It seemed impossible that he could survive many more hours, though. His neck was very badly cut. Large parts of his skin were gone on his head, his face, his back, his chest, a shoulder, a leg, an arm, a hand. And they had no medicine for him. They tied some cloths around his cuts but could do nothing more. They waited for him to die in the night.

But to everyone's surprise, he did not die that first night.

* The American West: the area west of the Mississippi River that is now part of the United States

4

She stood up on her back legs, two meters tall.

This was good news ... and bad.

What could they do with the dying man? There were Native American enemies all around them. It was too dangerous to stay in one place. Their boss, Andrew Henry, told them to make a bed for Glass with some long sticks. For two days they continued on their way, carrying Glass on this bed. But it was terribly painful for Glass, when he was awake. And it was terribly hard work for the men who were carrying him.

On the third day, Henry stopped his men. "We can't continue like this," he said. "We'll all be dead soon if we can't travel faster. I need two people to stay with Glass. When he's dead, you can come after us. I'll pay you well for your trouble."

Two men, Fitzgerald and Bridger, decided to stay with Glass. They badly wanted the money that Henry offered. They watched nervously as their other friends said goodbye.

After four scary days by Glass's side, their friend was getting worse, not better. But his heart was still going. Until his heart stopped, Fitzgerald and Bridger could not leave. And an attack by Native Americans was possible at any time.

"We should leave him," said Fitzgerald on the fifth day. "Our own deaths won't help Glass to live."

"But we can't just go," replied Bridger. "When he dies, we'll have to take all his things with us. If we don't have them, it'll be clear to everyone. They'll know that we didn't wait with him. And then we won't get our money."

"Then we'll have to take his things now," said Fitzgerald.

"But we can't leave him here without a gun!"

"He'll be dead soon. Dead men don't need guns."

They continued to discuss the matter for some time. Glass could not speak because of the great cut in his neck, but he could hear every word of their discussion. He waved his arms at his friends. "No!" he said with his eyes. "Don't leave me!"

But soon the two men picked up Glass's bag and his gun.

They moved his bed nearer to the river and put a coat over his bloody body. Then they disappeared.

Glass was very angry. Fitzgerald and Bridger were not just bad friends. They were thieves. "I'm not going to die until I get my gun back," he promised himself.

For four or five days he could not move. During that time he was robbed again, when wild animals took his coat. But then he started to feel stronger. From his bed, he put his hand into the river and got himself some water. He reached into the trees and picked some little fruits. But this was not enough. He lay on his bed, waiting for some luck.

It came. One day he woke up and saw a snake sleeping in the sun near his bed. Glass killed it by hitting it with a stone. Then he broke it into small pieces between two stones and ate it.

Stronger after this meal, he got up from his bed. It was time to get his gun back. He soon found that he could not walk. But he could pull and push himself along the ground with one arm and one leg. At first he could only go about fifty meters a day. Help was 320 kilometers away, along the river at Fort Kiowa. But Glass refused to believe that this goal was impossible.

As a younger man, Glass lived with Native Americans for a few years. He knew all the plants that made good food. He knew the best places to find birds' eggs on the ground, too. He was never hungry. Using his one good arm and one good leg, he was soon moving three or four kilometers a day.

One day he found wild dogs eating a dead animal. When their stomachs were full, Glass scared the dogs away. For the next few days he stayed by the dead animal. He ate, rested, and looked after himself. Slowly he was getting better. Only the cuts on his back were a worry. He could not reach them to clean out the insects inside.

When he started traveling again, he could walk. He carried a big stick. With this he could kill small animals in his path, so he could now eat plenty of meat. One day while he was looking for food, he met a group of Native Americans. Luckily they were friendly to white men. They cleaned the cuts on his back and took him to Fort Kiowa.

With a new gun on his back, Glass was soon on a boat to Fort Henry. He hoped to find Bridger, Fitzgerald, and his stolen gun there. But even now he was not out of danger. The boat was attacked by Native Americans and all the men on it were killed. Glass was lucky. At the time of the attack he was on land, looking for food.

Without a boat, Glass now had to reach Fort Henry, 400 kilometers away, on foot. But this was no problem for a man like Glass. After a month of walking through snow and ice, with no shelter at night, he found Andrew Henry and his men.

When the men first saw Glass, they were very scared. The person in front of them was very thin. He was like Glass but different. They knew from Bridger and Fitzgerald that Glass was dead. So who—or what—was this man?

Glass started to tell them his story. The men's fear left them, and they were soon welcoming Glass warmly. Only Bridger was silent. He felt terrible about leaving Glass alone. He felt terrible about his own lies. And he felt scared. What did Glass plan to do to him?

Glass looked at Bridger—nineteen years old and shaking with fear. He could not hurt this boy. But he wanted his gun.

"Fitzgerald has it," said Bridger. "But he isn't here."

For four more months, Glass looked for Fitzgerald. He thought about shooting him for his crimes. But Fitzgerald was a soldier now. When Glass finally found him, he was well protected. Murder was impossible. Glass shouted angrily at Fitzgerald, at his officers, and at the other soldiers. But when he left, he was a happy man. Over his shoulder he carried his favorite gun.

Under the Volcano

Johanna Beyerinck heard a great noise coming from the island of Krakatoa. It made her nervous.

Johanna Beyerinck heard a great noise coming from the island of Krakatoa.

Three months ago, Krakatoa was just an ordinary island. But then it suddenly started pouring out smoke. Strange noises were heard. People realized that the mountain on the island was a volcano. No one worried too much, though. There were other volcanoes in the area, and they were not often a problem.

But today the noises sounded different ... more dangerous.

Johanna Beyerinck and her husband Willem were Dutch, but they were living far from home on the island of Sumatra*. It was 1883, and Sumatra had a Dutch government at that time. Willem worked for the government in the small coastal town of Ketimbang. The Beyerincks lived very comfortably there, with plenty of Sumatran servants to look after their house and their three children.

On the beach, Willem watched the waves. They were much bigger than usual that Sunday evening, and were breaking many of the fishing boats on the sand. At eight o'clock, little pieces of volcanic rock started falling from the sky like rain. One of the waves reached the buildings next to the Beyerincks' home. It was time for Willem to find somewhere safer for his family.

There was a little house in the hills behind Ketimbang where the Beyerincks usually spent the hottest days of summer. Willem decided to take his wife and children there.

While Johanna was getting everyone ready for the long walk, some Sumatrans ran to her in fear. "The ocean has gone!" they cried. "There is no water now. Only sand."

Above the noise of the rocks raining on the roof, she heard another noise. It was coming from the ocean, and it was getting louder and louder. She pulled her youngest child to her and shouted to the others, "Come here! Everyone—together!"

A great wave crashed into the house.

Outside, Willem Beyerinck was safely up a tree. After the

---

* Sumatra: an island in south-east Asia, now part of Indonesia

wave fell back, he ran to the house. The buildings in the yard were washed away, and the stairs in the house were gone, too. But his family was safe, up on the first floor.

"I can't get up to you!" Willem called. "Jump, and I'll catch you. We're going now!"

Soon the Beyerincks and their servants were hurrying into the hills. Behind them the ocean made angry noises. They could not go the usual way, because the coast was too dangerous. They went through the forest. But it was dark and there was no path. They quickly got lost. Luckily they met some Sumatrans who were also running from Ketimbang. The Sumatrans helped everyone through the trees, one person holding onto the next. They reached the little house in the hills at about midnight.

The family and servants crowded into the simple shelter, but no one could sleep. The noises from Krakatoa were too loud. Outside, thousands of Sumatrans were also spending the night on high ground. They shook with fear and asked Allah for help.

Morning came. While the servants prepared some food, Johanna went outside. She looked around in fear. The ground was covered with ash and volcanic rock. There was an unnatural darkness, lit only by lightning and by thousands of strange tongues of fire on the ground.

She went back inside to eat. But after the meal, ash started flying up through the spaces in the wooden floor. Then everything went completely black, and everyone was thrown to the ground. Large pieces of rock fell through the roof, each piece bigger than the last. Johanna heard screams around her, and people shouting "Allah! Allah!" Then there were bodies on top of her, and kicking feet. But she could not hear her family. Johanna felt that there was no air in the house. She wanted to go outside but at first she could not move. Then, slowly, she made her way to the door. She could not find the steps.

11

She fell onto the hot ash on the ground outside. She started walking but her hair was soon caught in a burnt tree. As she pulled herself free, she noticed her skin. It was hanging heavily from her body, covered with thick ash. She thought at first that she was just dirty. She tried to clean herself. But the skin came off in big pieces. It hurt terribly. But her tired mind did not understand that she was badly burned.

Willem found her in this state. "Come inside," he said. "We should die together."

"Don't say that," she replied. "There will be rescuers here soon. They'll take us to the hospital."

"The hospital is probably destroyed," he said sadly.

Around them were the dead bodies of a thousand Sumatrans, About two thousand were still alive, but they were all terribly burned.

One of the servants brought Johanna her baby son. He seemed very thirsty, so she tried to give him some milk. Suddenly his body stopped moving. She listened to his chest. She could not hear his heart.

"His suffering has ended," she said calmly.

People around her started to cry for the dead child. But Johanna could not cry. Everything seemed unreal, like a bad dream.

The hours and days passed in that terrible darkness. News came on the Tuesday night that worse was coming. "You must leave this place," a Sumatran told the Beyerincks. "This mountain is a volcano, too, and it's going to kill you all!"

Willem and Johanna looked at the top of the mountain. There was a green light around it. Was it as dangerous as Krakatoa?

They did not wait to find out. With their two surviving children and their servants, they hurried down the hill toward Ketimbang.

They met some people coming from the town. "We got into the river to protect us from the ash rain," they said. "But Ketimbang is destroyed. The houses were broken by falling rocks, and almost everyone is dead. Some were killed by the burning ash, and others by houses crashing down on them."

Suddenly it started to rain again—not ash or rock, this time, but hot, wet earth. One of the servants was sent to get a table from the house in the hills. The two Beyerinck children were soon sheltering under the table. Their parents lay at each end to give them better protection.

When the rain stopped, they stood up. Johanna noticed something wonderful in the sky—a small circle of red light. It was Wednesday morning, and finally the sun was reaching through the clouds of ash. Slowly, the darkness of the last two days lifted. Sunlight!

Johanna looked toward Krakatoa. At first she could not understand what she was seeing. "Krakatoa has disappeared!" she cried.

It was true. The big island and its 800-meter high mountain were gone. There was just a small, low island there now. On Monday morning, the volcano of Krakatoa destroyed itself, making a noise louder than any other noise in recorded history. It was heard 4,600 kilometers away. Pieces of the volcano flew 15 kilometers up into the air. Other pieces fell into the ocean, making waves more than 36 meters high. These terrible waves washed away homes and people all along the south coast of Sumatra and the north coast of neighboring Java. Thirty-six thousand people lost their lives, and 165 towns were destroyed.

It took four more days for rescuers to reach the Beyerincks and the other survivors at Ketimbang. At first no boats could move through the water, because it was full of rock from the volcano, broken pieces of houses, and dead bodies. When the rescuers finally arrived, the survivors were very near to death. But unlike so many thousands of other people in the area, they were alive.

Escape from the Ice

It was a cold but sunny summer's day in January 1915. As the *Endurance* sailed through the icy water, the twenty-eight men on the ship felt excited. They were only a day away from the coast of Antarctica. From there, they planned to make the first trip in history from one side of Antarctica to the other.

But there was too much ice in the water. The ship had to stop. For a week, the men tried everything to break through the ice. But nothing worked. "I'm sorry, men," their boss, Ernest Shackleton, said finally. "We can't move the ship, and the Antarctic winter is coming. We'll have to wait on the ice until next spring. Then we can start traveling again."

This was terrible news. Spring was nine months away. Could they survive nine months on a big piece of ice that was moving slowly away from land? A lot of men died in the Antarctic. Were the men on the *Endurance* next?

Shackleton kept his men busy. No one had time to worry

There was too much ice in the water. The ship had to stop.

about their difficulties. First they had to build homes of ice next to the ship for their sixty-nine dogs. These special dogs from Canada were perfectly happy in the cold weather. The men took them out onto the thick ice for exercise every day, and soon loved them as pets. The men still lived on the *Endurance*, but they now called it "The Ritz," the name of an expensive hotel in London. Sometimes they killed animals for meat—for the dogs and for themselves. There were ball games and dog races on the ice. The men sometimes felt scared and bored, but they were facing the danger of their position bravely.

The sun disappeared from the sky on May 1st and the darkness of the Antarctic winter began. For seventy days there was no sunlight. The snow storms were terrible.

When spring finally arrived, worrying noises started to come from the ice. It was softer now, and it was moving. It was pushing harder and harder against the ship. Shackleton realized that the ship was breaking. In October he ordered his men to leave the *Endurance*. Without a ship, his dream of crossing Antarctica was impossible, too. Sad and afraid, Shackleton and his men put up tents for themselves on the ice.

But Shackleton did not have time to think about his broken dreams. He had other worries, and another goal. Without the protection of the ship, the lives of his men were now in very serious danger. "But I will bring them all home alive," he decided. "If I can do this, I'll make history."

The ice was always moving. They were now 1,900 kilometers from the place where the *Endurance* stopped eleven months earlier. They decided to go to the nearest place with food and shelter—Paulet Island, 550 kilometers to the north.

The dogs pulled the men's food and equipment across the ice toward Paulet Island. But the men had to pull the small boats from the *Endurance*. These boats were very heavy, and the ice was not smooth and flat. At the end of the first day, they were only two kilometers nearer to their goal.

"We can't leave the boats," Shackleton told his men. If the ice breaks under our feet, we can jump into them. Without them we have no hope of survival."

They continued, but they were moving too slowly. Shackleton soon realized that this plan could not work. There was still not enough open water to travel by boat. They had to find a thick piece of ice, put up their tents again, and wait.

They waited for many months. They were often wet and always hungry. Shackleton sadly ordered his men to kill the dogs. They were not useful now, and ate too much meat.

Finally, in April 1916, there were breaks in the ice and they could start sailing. The nearest land was now Elephant Island, 160 kilometers to the north. The men got into their three boats. Seven stormy days later, they reached the island.

They were on land for the first time in more than seventeen months. But they were not yet out of danger. Elephant Island was safer than the ice, but it was a cold, lonely place, with icy winds and very little shelter. The nearest people and homes were almost 1,300 kilometers across the stormy ocean, on the island of South Georgia.

Shackleton chose the three best sailors in the group to go there with him: Worsley, Crean, and McCarthy. He also chose the two men who were the most difficult: McNish and Vincent. Shackleton was leaving the other men on Elephant Island to wait for his return with a rescue ship. He did not want McNish and Vincent on the island, making trouble.

In their small open boat, Shackleton and the other five men sailed north through angry storms. Day after day, they were showered with water from the ocean. Their clothes and sleeping bags were always wet, and the salt ate into their skin. The water on the boat turned quickly to ice and became dangerously heavy for the boat. The men spent their days cutting the ice away. Again and again the waves almost

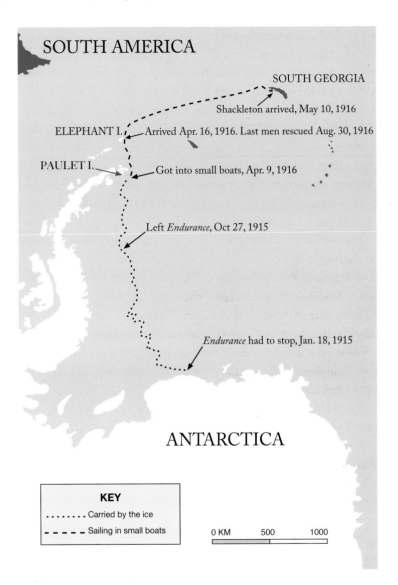

SOUTH AMERICA

SOUTH GEORGIA

Shackleton arrived, May 10, 1916

ELEPHANT I. — Arrived Apr. 16, 1916. Last men rescued Aug. 30, 1916

PAULET I. — Got into small boats, Apr. 9, 1916

Left *Endurance*, Oct 27, 1915

Endurance had to stop, Jan. 18, 1915

ANTARCTICA

KEY

. . . . Carried by the ice

– – – – Sailing in small boats

0 KM   500   1000

destroyed the boat, but the men were lucky. The boat survived.

It was Worsley's job to guide the boat toward South Georgia. But he had only very simple equipment, and the sun and stars were almost always covered in cloud. A small mistake in his measurements meant death for all of them, because there were no other islands in the area. By now there was no more fresh water on the boat and the men were very thirsty. They needed to find South Georgia very soon.

On the fourteenth day after leaving Elephant Island, they shouted excitedly. The coast of South Georgia was coming into view! But the men could find nowhere safe to land that evening. In the night, a storm carried them away from the coast. It was another two days before they finally landed.

They checked their position. More bad news! The nearest population on the island was 30 kilometers away in Stromness, on the other side of some high, snowy mountains.

After their weeks in the boat, McNish and Vincent were too weak to continue. McCarthy stayed with them, while Shackleton, Worsley, and Crean prepared for their climb into the mountains. They put sharp pieces of metal into the bottom of their boots, to bite into the snow and ice. They had a rope, a little stove, and some food, but no tents or sleeping bags.

They left in the morning. They climbed and climbed, then traveled downhill on their bottoms, like children. It was very dangerous, but it was faster and easier than walking. They walked through the night, with a full moon lighting their way. There were two stops for hot meals, but by 5 A.M. they were very tired. They sat down in a tight circle and rested.

Worsley and Crean were soon asleep. Shackleton knew that, in the cold, sleep could too easily become death. He woke up his friends. "It's time to go. You've had half an hour's sleep," he told them. In fact they were only asleep for five minutes.

In the morning they heard a wonderful sound. The factory at Stromness was calling its employees to work. They were almost at their goal. But danger still lay in front of them. On the way to Stromness, Shackleton fell into an icy lake. Later they all had to jump down a waterfall 10 meters high. Wet and shaking with cold, three men with long beards and dirty old clothes arrived in the little town.

"We've come from the other side of the island," said these strange-looking men.

"But that's impossible," was the reply. "No one has ever crossed those mountains."

Finally they were welcomed into the factory boss's warm home. There were tears and smiles as the men enjoyed a wash and shave, a hot cup of coffee, and some cake.

But they could not rest for long. Worsley went back with a rescue party for McNish, McCarthy, and Vincent on the other side of the island. Shackleton immediately started planning a rescue of the men on Elephant Island. In the following months, he tried three times to reach them in different boats. But there was thick ice all around the island, and rescue was impossible.

The men on Elephant Island continued to wait. They were living in a shelter built with piles of rock for walls and their two boats for a roof. They burned animal fat. One man lost his toes because of the terrible cold, but no one died.

By August, the men on Elephant Island were getting seriously worried. It was 105 days since they last saw Shackleton and the others. Where were they? It was probably time to send another boat in search of rescue.

Most of the men were in the shelter for lunch. Suddenly they heard a shout outside: "There's a ship!" It was true! There was a ship, and Shackleton was on it.

"Are you all well?" he shouted.

"All safe! All well!" they replied.

Everyone was soon on the ship and sailing north. After twenty-two months without news, their families finally heard from them. They were coming home.

133 Days on a Raft

"Jump!" said the ship's officer. Poon Lim looked at the rough water far below. He was not a good swimmer. "Jump!" repeated the officer. "Or you'll go down with the ship."

Poon jumped. Above and around him, the water was moving fast, pouring into the holes in the broken ship. He kicked and kicked but he was still underwater. His mouth opened, and filled with water and oil. Then, suddenly, he was pushed back up, into the air.

He coughed and coughed. Then he tried to look around. But at first he could not open his eyes. There was too much oil in them. He cleaned them with the saltwater, and finally he could see.

But he soon wanted to close his eyes again. His ship was not there. In its place, there were a few pieces of wood ... and a lot of dead bodies lying on top of the water.

It was 1942, and 25-year-old Poon Lim was a long way from his home in China. He started working as a servant on a British ship, the *Benlomond*, to escape attack from the Japanese in the Second World War. But on the *Benlomond* there was a different danger. The Germans were destroying all the British ships that they could find. They shot at the *Benlomond* on its way from South Africa to Dutch Guyana*, and only two minutes later the ship disappeared underwater. So now Poon was here, alone in the South Atlantic Ocean.

For three hours Poon was pushed around by the waves. He held onto a piece of wood. But it was difficult to keep his head above water. Then, as one wave carried him up, he saw one of the *Benlomond*'s life-saving rafts. It was a long way away. Could he reach it? He started swimming. Slowly, slowly, he got closer. At last he pulled himself onto it, tired but grateful.

★ Dutch Guyana: a country north of Brazil, now called Suriname

The raft was about two and a half meters square. In a little cupboard, he found some cans of cookies, some sugar and chocolate, and a metal bottle with 40 liters of water. That was enough food and drink to keep him alive for a month or more. "Someone will find me before that," he hoped.

He felt terribly cold, so he pulled off his wet clothes. Soon, feeling a little warmer, he went to sleep.

When he woke, the clothes were gone. He was angry with himself. What a stupid mistake! Under the hot sun, his unprotected skin burned badly. He lay in the raft, crying with pain and fear. But finally he ate, and immediately felt braver. In the little cupboard he found a piece of material, and with this he made a roof for his raft.

Day followed day. In his past life Poon was always happiest alone, but he was not prepared for the loneliness of the wide, empty ocean. He watched the fish. He sang Chinese songs to himself. But time passed very slowly.

Soon, though, his hopes were answered. A big ship came close. Poon waved his arms and shouted. He was sure that the pilot could see him. But no, the ship continued on its way. Another day, seven U.S. planes flew low above him, but again, he was not seen. He watched as the planes got smaller and smaller in the sky. His hopes of rescue disappeared with them.

When it was destroyed, the *Benlomond* was about 1,200 kilometers from the Brazilian coast. Poon knew that his raft was going slowly west. He realized that he had only one real hope of survival. He had to keep himself alive on the raft until it reached the coast of South America. So he had to get more to eat and drink.

He used the roof material to catch rainwater. He then poured it into his water bottle. And he decided to catch some fish. He made a knife with part of a food can. With this, he

21

cut out the wood around a small piece of metal in the raft. He pulled the metal with his teeth, harder and harder. The pain in his mouth was terrible, but finally the metal came out. He shaped it, then tied it to some rope. Now he had a fishing line.

With a small shellfish from the side of the raft on the end of his line, he caught his first fish. He ate it uncooked, but it did not taste good. He hung his next few fish in the sun before eating them. Dried fish tasted better and lasted longer. Soon he became very good at fishing and had enough food in his cupboard for many days.

But water was still a problem. When there was no rain, his bottle was soon empty. And sometimes there were storms. The waves crashed over the raft and saltwater mixed with his fresh water. Then he could not drink it and death seemed close. Sometimes he even had to drink his own urine.

After one storm, Poon saw a group of birds. He made a plan to catch one. He left out some fish. One of the birds smelled the fish and landed on his raft. Poon lay without moving. The bird started eating the fish. Suddenly Poon jumped onto it and broke its neck. He drank its blood thirstily. Then he ate it.

After 131 days on his raft, the water became browner. There were more birds, too. Poon felt sure that land was near.

He was right. On the 133rd day, he saw land—kilometer after kilometer of rain forest trees. Then he saw a small sail. He waved and jumped up and down. The fishing boat with the sail turned and came toward him. Rescuers, at last!

The family on the boat could not believe their eyes when they saw Poon. They gave him some food and took him to a hospital. He was in Brazil, at the mouth of the River Amazon.

He could walk without help. He was 13 kilos lighter than at the start of his terrible adventure, but after a few weeks in the hospital he was fit and healthy again.

After a few weeks in the hospital, he was fit and healthy again.

No one has survived longer than Poon's 133 days on a life raft. It is a world record. "I hope that no one ever has to break that record," he told the newspapers.

Plane Crash in the Rain Forest

Juliane Köpcke and her mother were finally on the plane, after a long wait at the airport in Lima, Peru.

It was 1971, and seventeen-year-old Juliane was enjoying a busy few days. Yesterday, her high school graduation party in Lima. Today, the flight to Pucallpa, a city in the middle of the rain forest. And tomorrow, Christmas Day. She wanted to spend the next few days with her father in the rain forest science center where he was working.

Juliane had the seat next to the window. Her mother was in the middle seat, and a fat man was asleep on the other side. Suddenly, thirty minutes into the flight, they flew into a storm. Juliane realized that it was a bad one. The plane started shaking and Christmas gifts fell out of the cupboards above the passengers' heads. Then the plane was hit by lightning. Juliane's mother saw that it was on fire. "This is the end!" she screamed.

After that, Juliane does not remember very much. The plane started going down, nose first. Then suddenly Juliane was outside the plane, falling in circles down toward the green trees of the rain forest. She was still in her seat, with two seats next to her. But the other seats were empty. Her mother and the fat man were not there.

She woke on the ground, under the group of seats, covered in dirty water. She tried to look around her. It was difficult because she could only open one of her eyes. Her glasses were lost, too, and her head hurt. But she soon realized that she was alone.

She tried to walk, but quickly fell to the ground. She sat up and checked her body. She had one useless eye, a broken shoulder, and deep cuts on her arm and her leg, but nothing more serious. It seemed almost impossible that she was alive.

But where was her mother? Juliane looked and looked

but at first there were no signs of the plane. Finally she saw three dead bodies covered in flies. Some Christmas gifts were hanging in the trees. Sadly she accepted that her mother was probably dead.

She found a bag of candy and a big Peruvian Christmas cake. The cake was wet and dirty. She tried some, but it tasted terrible. She quickly threw it back on the ground. Later, after days without food, she realized her mistake. But by then it was too late. The cake was many kilometers behind her.

She was sure that people were looking for the plane and for survivors. But the rescuers could not see through the trees of the rain forest to the ground below. How long before they found her? Too long, she decided. She had to walk through the rain forest to somewhere with people—that was her only hope.

She knew about rain forests. Both her parents were German scientists who studied rain forest animals. She grew up in Peru and her happiest days as a child were in the rain forest. But she did not know where she was. Which way should she go?

She remembered her father's words: "Streams run into rivers," he always said, "and people live and travel on rivers. You'll never be lost in the rain forest if you follow a stream."

She started walking along a stream, dressed in a short skirt and one summer shoe. The other shoe was lost in the crash. She hit the ground with a stick before every step. She did not want to put her foot on a snake. Insects were a problem, too. They bit her skin and flew into her cuts.

She ate the candy that she found near the dead bodies. She did not look for other food. She did not feel hungry.

After three days, she came to a narrow river. "No boats come this way," she decided. "I must continue."

She walked and swam in the river. She could hear planes

above her. Rescue planes! But they could not see her. After a few days the rescuers disappeared. "They've stopped looking for survivors now," she thought. She felt very alone.

There were a lot of crocodiles next to the river. They jumped into the water when Juliane came close. But she was not worried. She knew that the crocodiles in this area did not attack people. They were going into the water to hide. The sting rays in the river were much more dangerous. It was difficult to survive an attack by one of these. As she walked, she hit the bottom of the river in front of her with her stick. That way, the sting rays attacked the stick and not her.

Sometimes she tried to clean the cut in her arm, but it was getting worse every day. It was full of insects. "If I don't get the right medicine soon, I'll lose my arm," she thought.

After many days without food, she was getting weak. Sometimes she was unable to walk or swim. She just lay in the water, half asleep, and the river carried her along.

Ten days after the crash she came to a bigger river. There was a boat ... but was it real, or just a dream? She touched it. Yes! It really was a boat! Near it there was a path with a few small steps. Juliane was too weak to climb the steps. She tried again and again. After hours she was finally at the top, and there she found a small shelter.

She lay in the shelter that night, thinking about her next step. She decided not to take the boat. She was too weak to use it.

Suddenly she heard voices. Three woodcutters arrived at the shelter. They could not believe it when they saw Juliane. But they cleaned the cut on her arm, then took her in their boat to the nearest doctor, eleven hours away. After months in the hospital, she went home. She could only see out of one eye, but she was in good health. Of the ninety-two people on the plane, she was the only survivor.

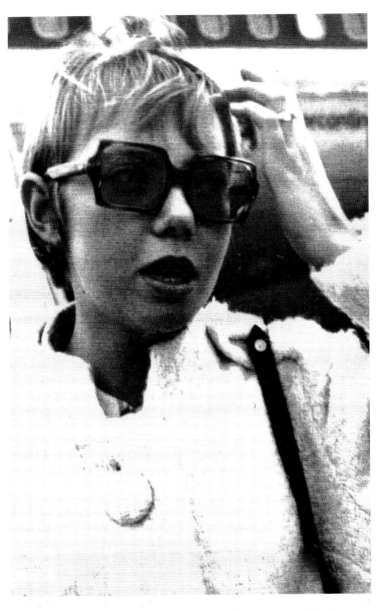

She could only see out of one eye, but she was in good health.

Murder in Rwanda

The Hutu killers came toward them with long knives.
Immaculée and the other Tutsis only had sticks and stones.

"Quickly, Immaculée," said her father. "You and Vianney must go to Simeon Murinzi's house. He is a good Hutu and a man of religion. You can stay with him until it's safe."

It was 1994. All around Rwanda, Hutus were murdering Tutsis. They destroyed Tutsi homes and then cut complete families to pieces. Ten thousand Tutsis were now outside Immaculée's home. They were hoping for help from her father, one of the most important Tutsis in the area. But her father had no answers to the Tutsis' problems.

For Immaculée, a 22-year-old college student, it was almost impossible to believe. There was a history of problems between Tutsis and Hutus, but in Immaculée's home town, Mataba, the two groups lived happily together. Until now.

Immaculée did not want to leave her parents. But in Rwanda a father's word was law. With a breaking heart, she kissed her parents and her big brother, Damascene. Then she and her younger brother Vianney ran to the home of Simeon Murinzi.

Murinzi welcomed them inside with a troubled smile. He had a lot of visitors, both Tutsis and Hutus.

Janet, Immaculée's best friend from school, was there. She was Hutu. Immaculée threw her arms around her. "My father wants me to stay here until it's safe," she said. "But why don't I go home with you? It'll be more fun if we can be together."

But Janet's eyes were cold. "Have you gone crazy, Immaculée?" she said. "We don't hide Tutsi insects in our house. I'm leaving." Then she walked angrily out of the room.

Immaculée could not believe it. She knew that the Hutu government and radio stations were telling a lot of lies about the Tutsis. But how could Janet change like this?

Immaculée and Vianney stayed the night at the Murinzis' house. She was woken by a visit from her brother Damascene.

"They've burned down our house!" he cried.

"What about Mom and Dad?" she asked. "Are they OK?"

"I don't know. They went off on Dad's motorcycle, but the killers are everywhere. The dead bodies of our friends are everywhere, too. This is the end, Immaculée. I can feel it."

He was planning to hide at the home of a Hutu friend. At the Murinzis' gate, brother and sister held hands. They could not think of anything to say. Damascene looked sadly at Immaculée, then pulled his hand out of hers and walked away.

The next day, it was Vianney's turn. The killers were looking for Tutsis everywhere—even in Hutu homes. "I'm going to take you to a safe hiding place," said Murinzi to Immaculée and five other Tutsi women in the house. "But your brother will have to go, Immaculée. I can't hide men here, too."

"No, please!" cried Immaculée. "They'll kill him!"

But Immaculée could not change Murinzi's mind. A few hours later, Vianney walked out into the darkness of the night.

Murinzi showed the women their new hiding place: a small bathroom about a meter square. Its door opened onto Simeon Murinzi's bedroom. There was a shower at one end, a toilet at the other, and a small, high window covered with red cloth. It seemed impossible to fit into this little room. But Murinzi packed them in tightly, their bodies pressed together.

"While you're in here, don't make a sound," he said. "Don't use the shower. Only use the toilet when the toilet on the other side of this wall is making a noise. No one must know that you are here. Not the servants. Not even my children. If anyone hears you, you will die."

He closed the bathroom door. The women tried to sit, but there was not enough space. The tallest people sat on the floor and the smaller ones sat on their knees. It was very hot and uncomfortable.

The next day, a big group of Hutu killers arrived at the Murinzis' house. They were Immaculée's friends and neighbors from Mataba, screaming for Tutsi blood.

They ran all around the Murinzis' house, looking in closets, in suitcases, in piles of earth in the yard ... and in Simeon Murinzi's bedroom. The Tutsis in the bathroom listened, weak with fear. But the killers did not open the bathroom door.

"Today we were lucky," Murinzi said later. "But they will come again. You can be sure of that."

Immaculée noticed a big cupboard in the bedroom. "Can we hide the bathroom door with that?" she suggested. Murinzi agreed to the idea. But was that enough to keep the Tutsis safe?

It was too dangerous for Murinzi to cook food for them. Late at night he usually brought a little food from the trash, but sometimes he brought nothing. Once a day the women stood up and moved a little, one person at a time. They used sign language, but they never spoke. It was too dangerous.

Day after day they heard screams outside, then laughing killers, then the sound of knives at work. One night a baby was crying, outside, alone. After murdering its mother, the killers were leaving it to die. The baby cried all night. In the morning it was quieter. By the end of the day there was no more crying. The baby was dead.

Sometimes Murinzi brought news, but it was never good. "The government has closed all the schools and stores until the job is done," he said one night. He looked very angry.

"What job?" the women asked.

"The job of killing Tutsis. They want every Tutsi dead."

Six weeks after the first killings, Murinzi brought two more Tutsi women to the bathroom. It was good news that other Tutsis were still alive. But the bathroom seemed even smaller.

By now they were all looking very thin. Without medicine, even regular illnesses became serious. They could not survive for many more weeks in that room.

For a change, Murinzi invited them into an empty bedroom in the middle of the night to watch a video. Even without the sound, it was wonderful to have a taste of ordinary life again!

But it was a big mistake. One of Murinzi's servants saw the blue light of the TV from outside the house. He told the Hutu killers. Soon the killers were back at the house.

"We know that you're here, Immaculée!" they called.

"This is where she was last seen," their boss shouted at Murinzi. "Where are you hiding her?"

They pulled out or knocked over almost everything in the house. Sometimes they were only centimeters away from the hidden Tutsis. But they failed to find the door to the bathroom.

A few days later, another servant suddenly asked to clean Murinzi's bathroom. Murinzi told him to clean a different room. But he realized that this was the end. The servant knew about the Tutsis' hiding place.

When the killings first started, all the international soldiers in Rwanda left the country in a hurry. Luckily, the French were now back. They were trying to protect any Tutsis who were still alive. Some French soldiers were near Mataba. Murinzi decided to take the women to them that night.

He finally told his children his secret. He needed their help. When they first saw the people in the bathroom, they stepped back in fear. These women looked like the living dead.

But soon everyone was outside the house. Murinzi and the men of his family walked on all sides of the eight Tutsi women, hiding them from view. When a group of sixty killers came toward them, their hearts raced. But the killers noticed nothing and continued on their way.

Too afraid to continue, Murinzi and his family said a quick

goodbye. The Tutsi women ran, unprotected now, to the tents of the French soldiers. There, they were welcomed kindly. After ninety-one days in the bathroom, it felt wonderful to be in the fresh air. They were given food—their first real food for months. But this was not the end of Immaculée's suffering.

There was news of her family. Her mother and father were dead. Vianney was dead. Damascene, too, was dead. They were just four of the 800,000 people that the Hutus killed in those terrible months.

Immaculée – a survivor

Desert Runner

Mauro Prosperi's feet kicked up the sand as he ran through the desert in Morocco. He had to run 84 kilometers that day in temperatures of 46°C, but he felt strong. He was in seventh place in the world's most difficult running race.

It was April 1994, and the fourth day of the Marathon des Sables*. Prosperi was racing against runners from all over the world—233 kilometers, in six days, across the Sahara Desert. The organizers gave them water. But if they wanted food or a sleeping bag, they had to carry their own. It was a race for the very fit, the very brave ... or the mad.

Thirty-nine year-old Prosperi worked as a policeman at home in Italy. He was also a great sportsman—an excellent runner, horserider, and swimmer. But nothing in his earlier life could prepare him for his next few days in the desert.

Around one o'clock, a sandstorm began. Prosperi continued running. He did not want other runners to go past him. But the wind was throwing sand hard in his face. He soon stopped, tied a towel round his face, and sheltered behind a plant.

When the storm finally ended, it was almost dark. Prosperi looked for the path, but he could not find it. He was angry with himself. Now he had no hope of winning the race. He got into his sleeping bag for the night. "The race organizers will find me tomorrow," he thought.

In the morning he climbed to the top of a hill. He could see nothing except endless sand. No runners, no race signs, no buildings. He had no idea where he was. And in this impossibly hot desert, he had almost no water.

But he felt sure that the race organizers were looking for

---

* *Marathon des Sables*: the French name for a very long race, on foot, across the sands of the Sahara Desert

him. He waited all day at the top of the hill. In late afternoon he heard the welcome sound of a rescue plane. But it flew straight past. The pilot did not see him.

It was a race for the very fit, the very brave ... or the mad.

The next morning he saw two large, ugly birds in the sky above him. "They're waiting for me to die," he thought. But he was not ready to die. He started walking.

Every hour, the sun got stronger and Prosperi felt weaker. Then he saw a building. It was empty, but he found three eggs there and ate them thankfully. He spent the rest of the day in the building, sheltering from the sun.

By evening, he was very hungry. There were bats in the roof of the building. Prosperi climbed up and caught two of them. He had a little gas stove but he decided not to use it. "Drink is more important now than food," he thought. "If I cook the bats, they will get drier." He sat in the half-darkness, eating the uncooked bats and drinking their blood. It was a terrible meal.

Just before the sun came up the next morning, Prosperi woke to the sound of another plane. "This is my last hope of rescue!" he thought. He made a fire with everything in his bag that could burn. Then he wrote in large letters in the sand: SOS⋆. But the plane continued on its way without stopping. "My life has ended," thought Prosperi.

He did not want to die a slow and painful death in the desert. After writing a letter to his wife, he cut his wrists. But his blood was thick. It did not pour out of the cuts in his wrists as he hoped. He could not kill himself.

He sat on the ground and cried. But after a few hours he started to think more clearly. He could see mountains about 30 kilometers away. Were these the mountains at the end of the race that one of the organizers described to him at the start? He decided to walk toward them.

For four days he traveled through the desert. He walked only in the early morning and the evening. In the heat of the day he rested in the shadow of rocks and trees. He drank

⋆ SOS: an international message that means *Help*

almost nothing—just the water that formed on plants and rocks at night. He always used a bottle when he urinated. Then he boiled the urine and mixed it with the dried food in his bag. He ate insects and plants. Once he killed a snake and ate that, too. Every evening he made a hole in the sand and slept inside it. This kept him warm during the cold nights.

Then, one day, he found a little pool. He threw himself into it and drank. He was immediately sick. His stomach could not hold anything. He drank again, more slowly this time—a small taste of water every ten minutes. All night he lay by the pool drinking. In the morning he felt much stronger.

There were no signs that people ever visited the pool. Prosperi filled his water bottle and continued on his way. He walked all day and all night but found nothing and no one.

The next morning, his luck finally changed. In the sand, he saw a shape left by a child's foot! He ran excitedly up the next hill, and there, below him, was a girl with her family's animals.

Prosperi ran to her, asking for help. But she ran away, screaming. "Do I look so very terrible?" he thought. He looked in the little mirror in his bag. His skin looked like a crocodile's. He learned later that he was 15 kilos lighter than at the start of the race. It was no surprise that the girl ran away.

But soon the girl came back with her grandmother, and Prosperi followed them to their home. His rescuers gave him tea and milk to drink. When the men of the family arrived, he was taken to the nearest town. He learned that he was in Algeria, 200 kilometers away from the race in Morocco.

After a long stay in the hospital, Prosperi went home to Italy. Four years later he returned to the *Marathon des Sables*. He has now completed the race six times. "I have terrible memories of those nine days lost in the Sahara," he explains. "But I have great memories, too. I'm a runner. And I love the desert."

ACTIVITIES

An Island of Sand

Before you read

1 Do you know any stories, fact or fiction, about people alone on small islands? Talk about one of them.

2 Which three of these will be important in this story about life on a desert island? Use the Word List at the back of the book to help you.

   a ship   a servant   turtles   bears   a fire   a volcano

While you read

3 Number these sentences in the right order, 1–6.

   a Serrano made a fire.   ......
   b Serrano swam to an island.   ......
   c Another sailor swam to the island.   ......
   d The other sailor died.   ......
   e The first ship passed the island but did not stop.   ......
   f A ship came to rescue Serrano.   ......

After you read

4 Describe three ways that Serrano used turtles.

5 Work in pairs. You are Serrano and the other sailor on the island. Act out one of these conversations.

   a You are meeting for the first time.
   b You live together. You are talking about the jobs that you must do. You are both angry.

Attacked by a Bear

Before you read

6 Has anyone ever stolen something from you? What was stolen? How did you feel?

7 The people in this story were in the West of the United States about two hundred years ago. Did a lot of white people live there at that time? What dangers did they face? What do you think?

While you read

8 Complete these sentences with the correct person or people. You can use an answer more than once.

Henry   Native Americans   Fitzgerald and Bridger   Glass

a .... killed a lot of Glass's friends.

b .... was attacked by a bear.

c .... was Glass's boss.

d .... took Glass's gun.

e .... pushed and pulled himself along the ground.

f .... helped Glass and took him to Fort Kiowa.

After you read

9 Work in pairs. Act out this conversation.

Student A: You are Glass at the end of the story. You are angry with Fitzgerald. Say why, and ask for the return of your gun.

Student B: You are Fitzgerald. Give reasons for your actions. Give back Glass's gun.

Under the Volcano

Before you read

10 Discuss these questions.

a Krakatoa (Krakatao in Indonesia) was a famous volcano. Do you know anything about its history?

b In what different ways can volcanoes kill people?

While you read

11 Number the problems, 1–4, in the order that they are first noticed by the Beyerincks.

a Rock and ash started falling from the sky.   ......

b There were dangerously big waves.   ......

c There was no sunlight.   ......

d Wet earth started falling from the sky.   ......

12 Are these sentences right or wrong?

    a People always knew that Krakatoa was dangerous.

    b The volcano killed one of the Beyerincks' children.

    c The ash from Krakatoa killed more people than the waves and falling rock.

13 Did the Beyerincks choose the right actions when they found themselves in danger? Give examples.

Escape from the Ice

Before you read

14 Would you like to visit the Antarctic, the coldest place on earth? Why (not)?

While you read

15 Match the names with the descriptions.

South Georgia .....   Paulet Island .....   Antarctica .....

Elephant Island .....   the *Endurance* .....

    a Shackleton and his men went there because they wanted to travel from one side of it to the other.

    b The men lived there before it was broken by ice.

    c Shackleton wanted to take his men there across the ice. But they couldn't reach it.

    d Shackleton and his men sailed there in three boats. There were no homes or people there.

    e On this island there were high mountains, a factory, and people who could help Shackleton.

After you read

16 Some business people use Shackleton as an example of a good boss. Why, do you think?

133 Days on a Raft

Before you read

17 The man in this story was alone on the ocean for 133 days. Do you enjoy being alone? How many hours or days can you spend alone before you want company?

18 Join the two halves of the sentences.

a	Poon's ship was attacked by	**1)**	a fishing boat.
b	On the raft, Poon found	**2)**	some U.S. planes.
c	Poon saw, but wasn't seen by,	**3)**	the Germans.
d	After a storm, Poon ate	**4)**	chocolate.
e	Poon was rescued by	**5)**	a bird.

After you read

19 Discuss what kept Poon alive on his raft.

Plane Crash in the Rain Forest

Before you read

20 Discuss these questions.

    a Do you know any stories of plane crash survivors? Where did they crash? How did they survive?

    b What are the main dangers for someone traveling in a rain forest?

While you read

21 Are these sentences right (✔) or wrong (✗)?

    a Juliane remembers the plane crash clearly. ......

    b She found her mother's dead body. ......

    c She knew a lot about rain forests. ......

    d She traveled along a river. ......

    e She found a boat and sailed it to the nearest town. ......

After you read

22 Work in pairs. Act out this conversation.

    Student A: You are Juliane's father. You think that your wife and daughter are dead.

    Student B: You are Juliane. Phone your father from the hospital. Tell him that you are OK, and about the crash and your days in the rain forest.

Murder in Rwanda

Before you read

23 Discuss these questions.

    a What do you know about Rwanda and its history?

    b Look at the photo on page 30. How many people can fit comfortably into a room of that size?

While you read

24 Complete the sentences with the correct names.

    a .... was Immaculée's older brother.

    b .... was Immaculée's younger brother.

    c .... was Immaculée's best friend.

    d .... hid Immaculée and some other Tutsi women in a bathroom at his house.

After you read

25 Why are these numbers important in the story?

    a 1994 **b** 8 **c** 91 **d** 800,000

Desert Runner

Before you read

26 Would you like to visit a desert? Why (not)?

While you read

27 Number these sentences in the right order, 1–6.

    a Prosperi completed the *Marathon des Sables*.   ......

    b A girl ran away from him.   ......

    c He tried to kill himself.   ......

    d Prosperi got lost in the Sahara Desert.   ......

    e He found a pool of water.   ......

    f He was taken to a hospital in Algeria.   ......

After you read

28 Answer the questions. Give reasons for Prosperi's actions.

    a Did he stop running when the sandstorm started?

    b Did he cook the bats before he ate them?

    c Did he walk all day in the desert?

d Did he sleep in holes in the ground?

e Did he wait by the pool until people found him?

Writing

29 Write a newspaper report about one of the stories in this book.

30 You are making a film about one of the survivors in this book. Write a plan for the first two minutes of your film.

31 Travel has changed a lot since the days of Serrano, Glass, and Shackleton. Is it better to be a traveler then or now? Give reasons.

32 You are one of the survivors in this book. You are worried that you are going to die. Write a letter to your family, saying goodbye.

33 Write a page of survival information for people who are in trouble in one of these places: the Antarctic, the desert, the rain forest, a raft on the ocean, a desert island.

34 Write to the makers of a TV program about the world's greatest survivors. Tell them about one survivor from this book who should be in the program. Give reasons.

35 You are organizing a survival skills course and you need some students. Write some information about the course: its goals and the different skills that are taught.

36 "Real survivors make their own luck." Discuss this, using examples from this book.